MICHAEL

BIG

BOOK OF
JOKES

by Michael Dahl, Jill L. Donahue, Mark Moore, and Mark Ziegler
illustrated by Anne Haberstroh, Ryan Haugen, Brian Jensen, Amy Bailey
Muelenhardt, Gary Nichols, and Ned Shaw

STONE ARCH BOOKS
a capstone imprint

Michael Dahl's Big Book of Jokes is published by Stone Arch Books,
A Capstone Imprint
1710 Roe Crest Drive
North Mankato, Minnesota 56003
www.mycapstonepub.com

Text © 2019
Illustrations © 2019 Stone Arch Books

Library of Congress Cataloging-in-Publication data is available on the Library of Congress website.
ISBN: 978-1-4965-8551-6 (paperback)

Art Director: **Kay Fraser**
Designer: **Emily Harris and Brann Garvey**
Production Specialist: **Jane Klenk and Kathy McColley**

Printed in China.
1667

TABLE OF CONTENTS

SCHOOL KIDDERS:
SCHOOL JOKES

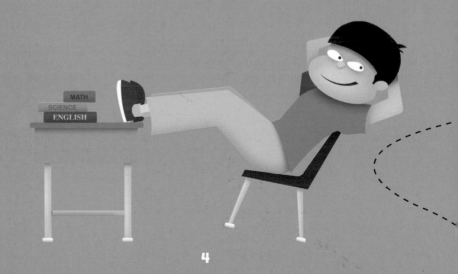

Who takes little monsters to school?

Their mummies.

Why was the broom late for school?

It overswept.

What's the difference between a school bus driver and a cold?

One knows the stops, and the other stops the nose.

What happened when the balloon got good grades?

It rose to the top of the class.

In what school do you have to drop out to graduate?

Sky-diving school.

What's the difference between a train and a teacher?

A train says, "Choo-choo," and a teacher says, "Spit out your gum!"

What kind of band doesn't make music?

A rubber band.

What do you call a student with a dictionary in his pocket?

Smarty pants.

What did the little turtles say to their teacher?

"You tortoise everything we know."

Teacher: Does anyone know which month has 28 days?

Student: All of them.

Why was the school clock punished?

It tocked too much during class.

Why do soccer players do well in school?

Because they really know how to use their heads.

What did the teacher do with the cheese's homework?

She grated it.

How did the music teacher unlock her secrets?

With piano keys.

Why did the computer have so many dents?

Because it was always crashing.

Why did the principal marry the janitor?

Because he swept her off her feet.

Why did the teacher send the clock to the principal's office?

Because it was taking too much time.

What did the paper say to the scissors?

"Cut it out!"

WHAT DID THE MAGNET SAY TO THE PAPER CLIP?

What kind of shoes do lazy students wear?

Loafers.

Why did the kids give Johnny a dog bone?

Because he was the teacher's pet.

Why did the music student bring a ladder to class?

Because the teacher asked him to sing higher.

What kind of socks do students in the school band wear?

Tuba socks.

Where's the best place to learn how to make ice cream?

At sundae school.

Why did Jimmy do so well on the geometry test?

Because he knew all the angles.

What's black and white and read all over?

The pages of a textbook.

Why did the school cook bake bread?

Because he kneaded the dough.

Why is history always getting harder?

Because new things happen every day.

Teacher: I thought I sent you to the back of the line?

Student: You did, but someone else was already there.

What do music teachers give their students?

Sound advice.

Mom: How do you like your astronomy class?

Son: It's looking up!

What do you call a duck that always gets good grades?

A wise quacker.

Teacher: The answer to the math question is zero.

Student: All that work for nothing!

Why was the school library so tall?

Because it had so many stories.

Why did the thermometer go to school?

It wanted to gain a degree.

Did the little tornado pass its math test?

Yeah. It was a breeze.

What did one math book say to the other math book?

"Boy do I have problems!"

Why did the student eat a dollar bill?

His mother told him it was for lunch.

What kind of fun do
math teachers have?

Sum fun.

Why did the girl bring a jump
rope to math class?

So she could skip the test.

WHY DID THE GIRL PUT ON LIPSTICK DURING CLASS?

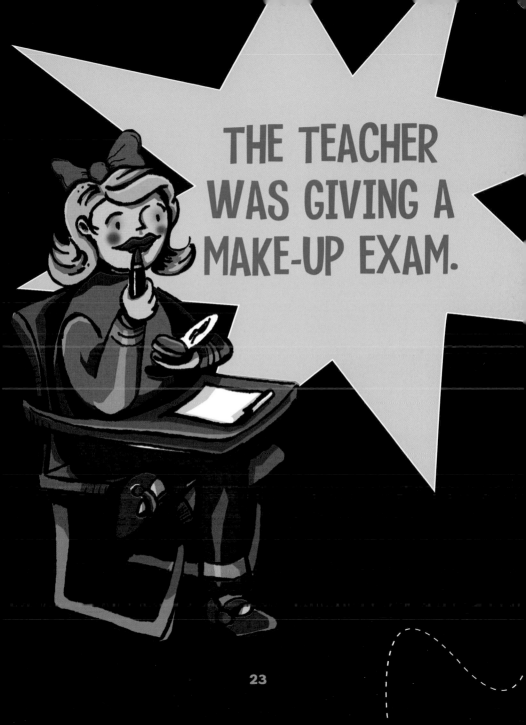

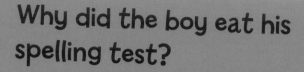

Why did the boy eat his spelling test?

Because the teacher said it was a piece of cake.

Why did the student swallow all his pennies?

The teacher said he needed more sense.

24

Why did the girls wear swimsuits to school?

They rode in a car pool.

Why was the jungle cat thrown out of school?

Because he was a cheetah.

What was the snake's favorite class?

Hisssssssssssssssssstory.

Why did the math teacher take a ruler to bed?

She wanted to see how long she slept.

What does a teacher get if he puts all of his students under a microscope?

A magnifying class.

How are elementary teachers like farmers?

They both help little things grow.

What was the witch's favorite subject in school?

Spelling.

Why did the nurse fail art class?

She could only draw blood.

Teacher: Why does the Statue of Liberty stand in New York Harbor?

Student: Because it can't sit down.

Who keeps track of all the meals in the school cafeteria?

The lunch counter.

28

What kind of pliers does a math teacher use?

Multipliers.

What animal makes the best teacher?

A skunk because it makes the most scents.

What runs all around the school without moving?

The fence.

Why did the student pour glue on her head?

To help things stick to her mind.

What kind of tree does a math teacher climb?

A geometry.

Teacher: Do you know the 20th president of the United States?

Student: No. We were never introduced.

Why is eight afraid of nine?

Because nine ate seven.

Teacher: Why is the Mississippi such an unusual river?

Student: Because it has four eyes and still can't see.

Why was the math book so sad?

Because it had so many problems.

Teacher: Why are you reading the last pages of your history book first?

Student: I want to know how it ends.

How do bees get to school?

They take the school buzz.

Why did the student keep a flashlight in his lunch box?

It was a light lunch.

Parent: Would you like a pocket calculator for school?

Child: I already know how many pockets I have.

What kind of snack does the computer teacher like?

Microchips.

School nurse: Have your eyes ever been checked?

Student: No, they've always been blue.

What did the sloppy student get on his math test?

Peanut butter and jelly.

Where does the third grade come after the fourth grade?

In the dictionary.

What do you call a basketball player's pet chicken?

A personal fowl.

What has 40 feet and sings?

The school choir.

Science teacher: What is a light year?

Student: A year with very little homework.

Where does success come before work?

In the dictionary.

Why did the teacher wear sunglasses?

Because his class was so bright.

How did the new teacher keep his students on their toes?

He raised all of the chairs.

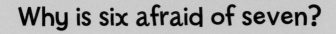

Why is six afraid of seven?

Because seven ate nine.

What did zero say to the number eight?

"Nice belt."

LUNCHBOX LAUGHS:
Food Jokes

Why did the cookie go to the doctor?

It was feeling crumby.

Why didn't the teddy bear eat dessert?

It was stuffed.

Why did the piecrust go to the dentist?

It needed a filling.

Why is corn such a friendly vegetable?

Because it's always willing to lend an ear.

What do ghosts eat for dessert?

Ice scream!

What food stays hot in the refrigerator?

Salsa.

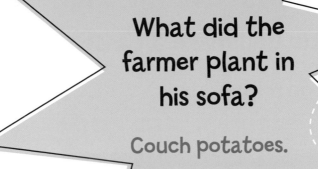

What did the farmer plant in his sofa?

Couch potatoes.

Why don't eggs tell jokes?

They'd crack each other up.

How do you make a casserole?

Put it on roller skates.

What did the soda say to the bottle opener?

"Can you help me find my pop?"

Why are strawberries such bad drivers?

They always get stuck in a jam.

Where do bakers keep their dough?

In the bank.

Why did the waitress walk all over the pizza?

Because the customer told her to step on it.

What did the plate say to the tablecloth?

"Lunch is on me."

What kind of lunch does a cheetah eat?

Fast food.

What did the hot dog say when it crossed the finish line?

"I'm the wiener!"

What did the astronaut put in his sandwich?

Launch meat.

Why did the orange lose the race?

It ran out of juice.

What do you use to fix a broken ketchup bottle?

Tomato paste.

What kind of fruit is never lonely?

Pears.

Why didn't the raisin
go to the dance?

It couldn't find a date.

What do frogs eat with their
hamburgers?

French flies.

Why did the little cookie cry?

His mother had been a wafer so long.

What vegetable do you get when an elephant walks through your garden?

Squash.

What do cheerleaders drink before a game?

Root beer!

Why did the doughnut maker sell his store?

He was tired of the hole business.

Why couldn't the monkey eat the banana?

Because the banana split.

Where do smart hot dogs end up?

On the honor roll.

What did the gingerbread boy use to make his bed?

Cookie sheets.

What is the worst kind of cake to have?

A stomach cake.

Why did the boy stare at the can of orange juice?

It said concentrate.

How is a baseball team like
a pancake?

They both need a good batter.

How do strawberries
greet each other?

Strawberries shake.

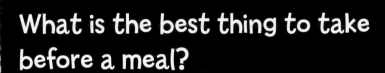

What is the best thing to take
before a meal?

A seat.

Why do crazy people like to eat cashews?

Because they're nuts.

How many rotten eggs does it take to stink up a kitchen?

Quite a phew.

What kind of food is good for your eyes?

Seafood.

Why did the banana
make so many friends?

Because he had a peel.

What do you get when you cross
a cow with a duck?

Milk and quackers.

Why did the sesame seeds get dizzy?

They were on a roll.

What did the hamburgers name their daughter?

Patty.

What do porcupines like to put on their hamburgers?

Sweet prickles.

What kind of shoes can you make from bananas?

Slippers.

GOOFBALLS:
Sports Jokes

What kind of hair do surfers have?

Wavy.

Why wouldn't they let the baby play basketball?

She wouldn't stop dribbling.

Why did Cinderella's team lose the volleyball game?

Because the coach was a pumpkin.

What is the hardest thing about sky diving?

The ground.

What color is a hockey score?

Goaled.

Why did the bowling pins refuse to stand up?

They were on strike.

Why did the golfer always wear two pairs of pants?

In case he got a hole in one.

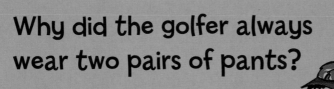

Why is a soccer stadium the coolest place in the world?

Because it's full of fans.

What does a runner lose when he wins a race?

His breath.

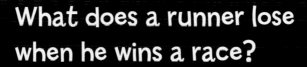

What is the quietest sport to play?

Bowling because you can hear a pin drop.

What is the loudest sport to play?

Tennis because players always raise a racket on the court.

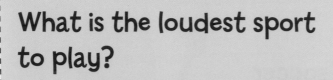

What has 18 legs and catches flies?

A baseball team.

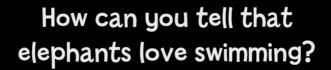

How can you tell that elephants love swimming?

Because they never take their trunks off.

What's the difference between a dog and a basketball player?

One drools and one dribbles.

Where do golfers go after a game?

To a tee party.

What do you call a girl who's good at catching fish?

Annette.

Why did the tennis player always carry a flashlight?

Because he lost all his matches.

What has wings and a skateboard?

Tony Hawk.

Why should you be careful playing sports in the jungle?

Because it's full of cheetahs.

Why did the frog try out for the baseball team?

He liked catching pop flies.

What do you call a pig that knows karate?

A pork chop.

What is a swimmer's favorite game?

Pool.

Did you hear about the race between the lettuce and the banana?

The lettuce was ahead.

Why do artists never win when they play soccer?

The game always ends in a draw.

What football team travels with the most luggage?

The Packers.

Why did the chicken cross the basketball court?

It heard the referee calling fowls.

WHY DID THE SOCCER BALL QUIT THE TEAM?

IT WAS TIRED
OF GETTING
KICKED AROUND.

What is an electric eels favorite football team?

The Chargers.

Where can you find the largest diamond in the world?

On a baseball field.

What kind of insect is bad at football?

A fumble bee.

What's the best thing for joggers to drink?

Running water.

Why did the softball player take her bat to the library?

Her teacher told her to hit the books.

Why do the fastest bowlers make the most strikes?

They have no time to spare.

Why didn't the dog want
to play soccer?

Because he was a boxer.

Why was Cinderella thrown off
the school's soccer team?

Because she ran away from the ball.

Why did the jogger
look so angry?

Because she was a
cross-country runner.

How is a scrambled egg like a bad football team?

They both get beaten.

What did the right soccer shoe say to the left soccer shoe?

Between us, we're gonna have a ball!

Why shouldn't you tell a joke when you are ice skating?

The ice might crack up.

How do fireflies start a race?

Someone shouts, "Ready. Set. Glow!"

Why did the football coach send in his second string?

So he could tie up the game.

Why did the volleyball coach want the waitress to join the team?

He heard she was a good server.

Why can't you go fishing if your watch is broken?

You won't have the time.

What is a runner's favorite subject?

Jography.

What did the basketball player wear to the school dance?

A hoop skirt.

How are peaches and racetracks alike?

They both have pits.

What kind of cats like to go bowling?

Alley cats.

What is the best way to win a race?

Run faster than everybody else.

What did the baseketball say to the player?

You've really got me going through hoops for you.

What is the best advice to give a young baseball player?

If you don't succeed at first, try second base.

Why did the basketball player cancel his trip?

He didn't want to get caught traveling.

Why did the golfer bring a cage to the golf course?

She was hoping to get some birdies.

Why did the exterminator hire a bunch of outfielders?

He needed people who were good at catching flies.

What kind of tea do football players avoid?

Penalty.

What is the biggest team in the NFL?

The New York Giants.

GIGGLE BUBBLES:

UNDERWATER JOKES

Where do mummies like to swim?

In the Dead Sea.

What do killer whales eat for dinner?

Fish and ships.

What did one ocean say to the other ocean?

"Nice to sea you!"

How did the oyster call his friends?

He used his shellphone.

What do you call a baby whale?

A little squirt.

How can you tell the sailboat is in love with the island?

It hugs the shore.

What's the difference between a piano and a fish?

You can tune a piano, but you can't tuna fish.

How much does it cost for a pirate to get his ears pierced?

A buccaneer.

What type of fish comes out at night?

A starfish.

How can you tell if an octopus parked in your driveway?

From the squid marks.

Why didn't the crab share his toys with his little brother?

Because he was shellfish.

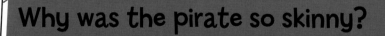

Why was the pirate so skinny?

Because he had a sunken chest.

Why was the mother octopus so upset?

All her kids needed new shoes.

How did the ocean explorer know he had discovered land?

He was shore of it.

WHAT DO YOU CALL A WHALE IN A BUS?

Why couldn't the sailor play cards?

Because the crew was sitting on the deck.

What do you do with a blue whale?

Try to cheer him up!

Why is a pirate ship a good place to buy stuff?

Because it has a big sail.

Why are fish easy to weigh?

They come with their own scales.

What bus crossed the ocean?

Columbus.

What happens when you throw a blue rock into the Red Sea?

It gets wet!

How do you close an envelope underwater?

With a seal.

What types of little cars do fish like to race?

Go-carps!

What fish prowls in the jungle?

A tiger shark.

What sits on the bottom of the ocean and shivers?

A nervous wreck!

Where do pirates like to hang out?

At the ARRRRcade.

What do you call a seabird's date?

His gullfriend.

WHAT'S BEHIND A PIRATE'S PATCH?

HIS AYYYYYYYYYYY, MATEY!

What kind of ships
carry vampires?

Blood vessels.

What's the best day
to go to the beach?

Sunday.

What kind of hair does the
ocean have?

Wavy.

Why are fish so smart?

Because they live in schools.

Why is it impossible to starve on a desert island?

Because of all the sand which is there.

What do you get when you mix an electric eel with a squid?

A shocked-opus.

What kind of fish
likes to tell jokes?

Clownfish.

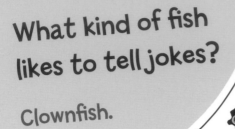

What kind of waves
wash up on the shore
of a tiny island?

Microwaves.

WHAT KIND OF FISH DO PIRATES HIDE IN TREASURE CHESTS?

GOLDFISH.

ROARING WITH LAUGHTER:

ANIMAL JOKES

What do you get when you put a turkey in the freezer?

A brrrrrrrrrd.

What do you get if you cross a bumblebee with a doorbell?

A humdinger!

Why did the snowman call his watchdog Frost?

Because Frost bites!

Why did the pelican get kicked out of the hotel?

It had a big bill.

Why did the bee trip over the flower?

It was a stumblebee.

What does a cow read in the morning?

The moospaper.

What do you get when you cross a duck with an alligator?

A quackodile.

Where did the cow go on the weekend?

To the mooovies.

How did the little fish get to school?

It took the octobus.

What kind of snake is good at cleaning cars?

A windshield viper.

What do you call a camel at the North Pole?

Lost!

What time is it when an elephant sits on a fence?

Time to fix the fence!

What do polar bears eat for lunch?

Icebergers.

What's big and gray and has lots of horns?

An elephant marching band.

WHAT KIND OF ANT IS GOOD AT MATH?

What do chickens do
on Valentine's Day?

They give each other pecks.

What did one bee say to the
other bee on a hot summer day?

"Sure is swarm, isn't it?"

What did the pony say when it had
a sore throat?

"Sorry, but I'm a little horse."

What goes "zzub zzub"?

A bee flying backwards.

What is the biggest ant in the world?

An elephant.

What follows a lion wherever it goes?

Its tail.

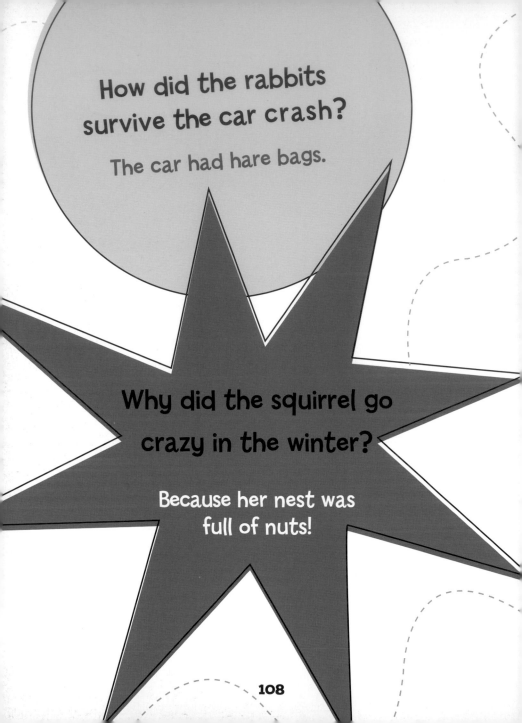

How did the rabbits
survive the car crash?

The car had hare bags.

Why did the squirrel go

crazy in the winter?

Because her nest was
full of nuts!

What do you call a crate full of ducks?

A box of quackers.

Why did the mole dig a tunnel into the bank?

To burrow some money.

How do rich birds make their money?

They invest in the stork market.

Why do turkeys always lose at baseball?

They can only hit fowl balls.

What kind of lions live in your front yard?

Dandelions.

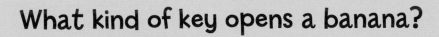

What kind of key opens a banana?

A monkey.

What did the little centipede
say to his mother when they
went shopping?

"I need a new pair of shoes.
And a new pair of shoes.
And a new pair of shoes . . ."

Why was the rooster all wet?

He was covered with cock-a-doodle dew.

What did the duck say when
she bought some lipstick?

Put it on my bill.

WHAT DO YOU CALL
A CHICKEN THAT LIKES
TO EAT CEMENT?

What do you call a crazy chicken?

A cuckoo cluck.

How did the grizzly catch a cold?

He walked outside with just his bear feet.

What did the cow ride when her car broke down?

A mootorcycle.

What do chickens eat at birthday parties?

Coopcakes.

Where do cows go in a rocket ship?

To the moooooon.

What do rabbits use to make their ears look nice?

Hare spray.

What do bees
wear when they
go to work?

Buzzness suits.

When dolphins play football, how do
they know which team gets the ball?

They flip for it.

Why do mother kangaroos hate
rainy days?

Because the kids have to play inside.

What kind of airplane do elephants ride in?

Jumbo jets.

Why don't animals play cards in the jungle?

There are too many cheetahs.

Why do birds fly south in the winter?

It's too far to walk.

What is the best kind of computer bug to have?

A spider. They make the best websites.

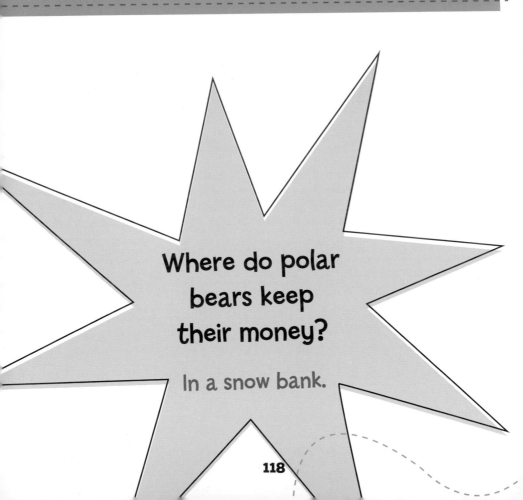

Where do polar bears keep their money?

In a snow bank.

How did the flea travel
from dog to dog?

It went itch-hiking.

Why did the crow perch on
the telephone wire?

He was going to make a
long-distance caw.

LAUGHS ON A LEASH:

PET JOKES

How can you tell if a snake
is a baby?

It has a rattle.

What did the dog
say when he sat
on sandpaper?

Ruff! Ruff!

Why did the little girl make her
pet chicken sit on the roof?

She liked egg rolls.

What kind of dog likes flowers?

A budhound.

Why do dogs have such big families?

Because they each have four paws.

What kind of dog wears a uniform and a badge?

A guard dog.

Why do baby skunks
make the worst pets?

They're always little stinkers.

What do you get when you put
a kitten in the copy machine?

A copycat.

Where do dogs go when they
lose their tails?

A retail store.

What do you get when you cross a canary with a snake?

A sing-a-long.

What pet comes with its own mobile home?

A turtle.

Why did the cowboy buy a dachshund?

Everybody told him to "get a long, little doggie."

What type of music do bunnies play at parties?

Hip-hop,

Why don't dogs make good dancers?

Because they have two left feet!

DID YOU HEAR ABOUT THE GOLDFISH WHO BECAME A QUARTERBACK?

Why did the puppy bite the man's ankle?

Because it couldn't reach any higher.

What kind of coat does a pet dog wear?

A petticoat.

Why is a group of puppies called a litter?

Because they mess up the whole house.

What do you get if your cat drinks lemonade?

A sour puss.

Why did the cat buy a computer?

So he could play with a mouse of his very own.

Why did the dog sleep under the car?

He wanted to wake up oily.

How do you spell "mousetrap" with just three letters?

C-A-T.

What do you call kittens that like to bowl?

Alley cats.

What do you call young dogs that play in the snow?

Slush puppies.

What did the hungry dalmatian say after a meal?

"That hit the spots!"

How many pet skunks do you have?

Quite a phew!

What do you give a pet rabbit for dessert?

A hopsicle.

What kind of dog can cook dinner for its owner?

An oven mutt.

What is a polygon?

When your pet parrot flies out of its cage.

Why did the kitten put the letter "M" into the freezer?

To turn some ice into mice.

What did the girl do when she found her pet dog eating the dictionary?

She took the words right out of his mouth.

What kind of dog is like a short skirt?

A peekin' knees.

What pet fish are the most expensive?

Goldfish.

Why did the boy take a bag of oats to bed?

To feed his nightmare.

What kinds of beds do fish sleep on?

Waterbeds.

What do you call a koala without any socks on?

Bearfoot.

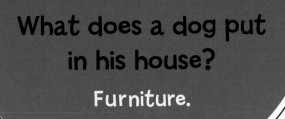

What does a dog put
in his house?

Furniture.

How did the girl talk
to her pet fish?

She dropped it a line.

How can you tell that carrots are
good for your eyes?

Because rabbits never wear glasses.

What do you give a dog with a fever?

Mustard. It's the best thing for a hot dog.

Why are some fish found at the bottom of the ocean?

Because they dropped out of school.

What do you get when you cross an elephant with a goldfish?

Swimming trunks.

What do frogs like to drink in the winter?

Hot croako.

Why are mice so noisy after they take a bath?

They're squeaky clean.

What do cats drink on hot summer days?

Miced tea.

Which side of a cat has the most fur?

The outside!

What did the dog say about his day in the woods?

"Bark, bark, bark, bark . . ."

WHAT DO DOGS LIKE TO EAT FOR BREAKFAST?

POOCHED EGGS.

What kind of pet can you stand on?

A carpet.

What do mice do when they're at home all day?

Mousework.

What's the best time to buy a pet canary?

When it's going cheep!

CHEEP!

What kind of pet can tell time?

A watchdog.

Mom: Why is your pet bunny so unhappy?

Emily: It's having a bad hare day.

Why can't dalmatians hide from their owners?

They're always spotted.

Why did the girl oil her pet mouse?

It squeaked.

Police officer: Young man! What is your dog doing in the street?

Boy: About seven miles an hour.

How do rabbits play the piano?

They play by ear.

Why is an octopus such a sweet pet?

It's covered with suckers.

143

ZOODLES:
ANIMAL RIDDLES

What side of a chicken has the most feathers?

The outside.

What do chimpanzees eat for a snack?

Chocolate chimp cookies.

What kind of pigs do you find on the highway?

Road hogs.

How can you tell when it's raining cats and dogs?

When you step into a poodle.

What do you call a crab that plays baseball?

A pinch hitter.

Where do sheep go for haircuts?

The BAA-BAA shop.

What kind of dog has no tail, no nose, and no fur?

A hot dog.

What happened when the bee telephoned his friend?

He got a buzzy signal.

What do you call a hot and noisy duck?

A firequacker.

What animal talks the most?

A yak.

What school contest did the skunk win?

The smelling bee.

What pet makes the loudest noise?

A trumpet.

What kind of vitamins do fish need?

Vitamin sea.

What do you call the top of a dog house?

The woof.

Who steals soap from the bathroom?

The robber duckie.

WHAT DID THE BANANA
DO WHEN IT SAW
THE HUNGRY MONKEY?

NOTHING. THE BANANA SPLIT.

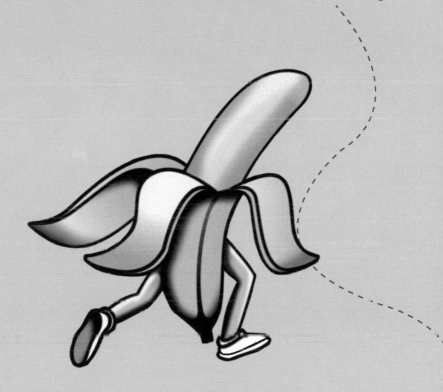

KNOCK
YOUR
SOCKS
OFF

Knock, knock.

Who's there?

Ice cream.

Ice cream who?

I scream, you scream,
we all scream for ice cream!

Knock, knock.

Who's there?

Henrietta.

Henrietta who?

Henrietta whole cake!

Knock, knock.

Who's there?

Champ.

Champ who?

Champoo your dog.
He's got fleas.

Knock, knock.

Who's there?

Freeze.

Freeze who?

Freeze a jolly good fellow.

KNOCK, KNOCK.

WHO'S THERE?

DORIS.

DORIS WHO?

DORIS LOCKED, THAT'S WHY I'M KNOCKING!

Knock, knock.

Who's there?

Amos.

Amos who?

A mosquito bit me.

Knock, knock.

Who's there?

Annie.

Annie who?

Annie bit me again!

Knock, knock.

Who's there?

Dishes.

Dishes who?

Dishes your friend,
so open the door.

Knock, knock.

Who's there?

Elsie.

Elsie who?

Elsie you later.

Knock, knock.

Who's there?

Little old lady.

Little old lady who?

I didn't know you could yodel!

Knock, knock.

Who's there?

Catsup.

Catsup who?

Catsup in the tree!

Knock, knock.

Who's there?

Harry.

Harry who?

Harry up and answer the door!

Knock, knock.

Who's there?

Abby.

Abby who?

Abby stung me on the nose.

Knock, knock.

Who's there?

Tennis.

Tennis who?

Tennis five plus five.

Knock, knock.

Who's there?

Butter.

Butter who?

Butter not tell,
it's a secret!

Knock, knock.

Who's there?

Yule.

Yule who?

Yule never know unless you
open the door.

KNOCK, KNOCK.

WHO'S THERE?

COWS GO.

COWS GO WHO?

NO, COWS GO "MOO."

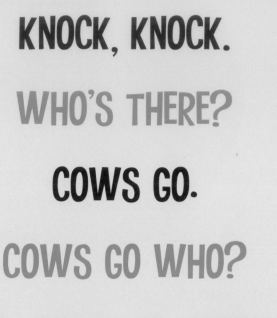

Knock, knock.

Who's there?

Hutch.

Hutch who?

Please cover your mouth
when you sneeze.

Knock, knock.

Who's there?

Anita.

Anita who?

Anita tissue.

Knock, knock.

Who's there?

Peeka.

Peeka who?

Peeka boo, of course.

Knock, knock.

Who's there?

Four eggs.

Four eggs who?

Four eggsample.

Knock, knock.

Who's there?

Cash.

Cash who?

I didn't realize you were a nut!

Knock, knock.

Who's there?

Eskimo.

Eskimo who?

Eskimo questions, and I'll tell you no lies.

Knock, knock.

Who's there?

Weasel.

Weasel who?

Weasel while you work!

Knock, knock.

Who's there?

Heaven.

Heaven who?

Heaven you heard enough
knock-knock jokes?

Knock, knock.

Who's there?

Hi.

Hi who?

Hi ho! Hi ho! It's off to work we go!

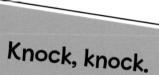

Knock, knock.

Who's there?

Tori.

Tori who?

Tori I bumped into you.

Knock, knock.

Who's there?

Megan.

Megan who?

Megan a cake. Do you have any eggs?

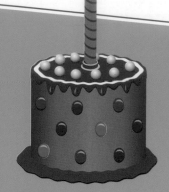

Knock, knock.

Who's there?

Juicy.

Juicy who?

Juicy who threw that snowball at me?

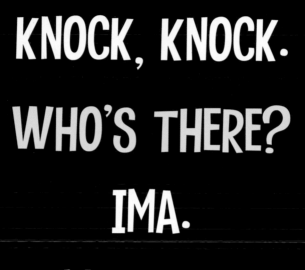

KNOCK, KNOCK.

WHO'S THERE?

IMA.

IMA WHO?

IMA GONNA HUFF AND
PUFF AND BLOW THIS
HOUSE DOWN!

KNOCK, KNOCK.

WHO'S THERE?

DAKOTA.

DAKOTA WHO?

Knock, knock.

Who's there?

Turnip.

Turnip who?

Turnip the heat, it's cold in here.

Knock, knock.

Who's there?

Handsome.

Handsome who?

Handsome of those cookies to me.

Knock, knock.

Who's there?

Ben.

Ben who?

Ben knocking so long my hand hurts!

Knock, knock.

Who's there?

House.

House who?

House it going?

Knock, knock.
Who's there?
Water.
Water who?
Water you doing at my house?

Knock, knock.
Who's there?
Wooden shoe.
Wooden shoe who?
Wooden shoe like to know?

Knock, knock.

Who's there?

Adam.

Adam who?

Adam up, and tell me the score.

Knock, knock.

Who's there?

Statue.

Statue who?

Statue making all that noise?

Knock, knock.

Who's there?

Queen.

Queen who?

Queen as a whistle!

Knock, knock.

Who's there?

Ivan.

Ivan who?

Ivan my money back.

Knock, knock.

Who's there?

Alpaca.

Alpaca who?

Alpaca the lunch for the picnic.

Knock, knock.

Who's there?

Ketchup.

Ketchup who?

Ketchup with me, and I'll tell you.

Knock, knock.

Who's there?

Radio.

Radio who?

Radio not, here I come.

Knock, knock.

Who's there?

Wah.

Wah who?

Well, you don't have to get so excited about it!

Knock, knock.

Who's there?

Dozen.

Dozen who?

Dozen anybody ever answer the door?

Knock, knock.

Who's there?

Tish.

Tish who?

Why yes, I'd love a tissue.

179

KNOCK, KNOCK.

WHO'S THERE?

DEWEY.

DEWEY WHO?

DEWEY HAVE TO KEEP LISTENING TO THESE KNOCK-KNOCK JOKES?

Knock, knock.

Who's there?

Luke.

Luke who?

Luke out!

Knock, knock.

Who's there?

Clair.

Clair who?

Clair the way, I'm coming through!

Knock, knock.

Who's there?

Avenue.

Avenue who?

Avenue heard me knocking all this time?

Knock, knock.

Who's there?

Roach.

Roach who?

Roach you a letter, but you never wrote back.

Knock, knock.

Who's there?

Pasture.

Pasture who?

Pasture bedtime, isn't it?

Knock, knock.

Who's there?

Tuba.

Tuba who?

Tuba toothpaste.

Knock, knock.

Who's there?

Justin.

Justin who?

Justin time for dinner.

Knock, knock.

Who's there?

Darrel.

Darrel who?

Darrel never be another you.

Knock, knock.

Who's there?

Les.

Les who?

Les hear some more jokes!

Knock, knock.

Who's there?

Summer.

Summer who?

Summer funny jokes and summer not.

KNOCK, KNOCK.

WHO'S THERE?

GORILLA.

GORILLA WHO?

GORILLA CHEESE SANDWICH
FOR ME PLEASE.

Knock, knock.

Who's there?

Broken pencil.

Broken pencil who?

Who cares. It's a pointless joke.

Knock, knock.

Who's there?

Watson.

Watson who?

Watson TV tonight?

Knock, knock.

Who's there?

General Lee.

General Lee who?

General Lee I do not tell jokes.

Knock, knock.

Who's there?

Colleen.

Colleen who?

Colleen up your room. It's a mess!

Knock, knock.

Who's there?

Thumping.

Thumping who?

Thumping creepy is crawling up my leg!

Knock, knock.

Who's there?

Isabelle.

Isabelle who?

Isabelle out of order? I had to knock.

Knock, knock.

Who's there?

Boo.

Boo who?

Why are you crying?

Knock, knock.

Who's there?

Snow.

Snow who?

Snowbody here but me!

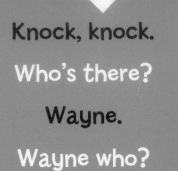

Knock, knock.

Who's there?

Wayne.

Wayne who?

Wayne, Wayne, go away.
Come again another day.

Knock, knock.

Who's there?

Butter.

Butter who?

Butter bring an umbrella.
It looks like rain.

Knock, knock.

Who's there?

Sarah.

Sarah who?

Sarah piece of pizza left?

Knock, knock.

Who's there?

Oswald.

Oswald who?

Oswald my gum!

Knock, knock.

Who's there?

Justin.

Justin who?

Justin the neighborhood, and thought I'd drop by.

Knock, knock.

Who's there?

Alma.

Alma who?

Alma candy's gone.

Knock, knock.

Who's there?

A herd.

A herd who?

A herd you were home, so I came over.

195

Knock, knock.

Who's there?

Shirley.

Shirley who?

Shirley you know more good jokes!

Knock, knock.

Who's there?

Juana.

Juana who?

Juana see a movie tonight?

Knock, knock.

Who's there?

Ben.

Ben who?

Ben looking all over for you.

Knock, knock.

Who's there?

Zombies.

Zombies who?

Zombies make honey,
and zombies don't.

Knock, knock.

Who's there?

Beehive.

Beehive who?

Beehive yourself, or you'll get hurt!

Knock, knock.

Who's there?

Omar.

Omar who?

Omar goodness, wrong door! Sorry!

Knock, knock.

Who's there?

Ach.

Ach who?

Bless you!

Knock, knock.

Who's there?

Anita.

Anita who?

Anita one more minute to get ready.

KNOCK, KNOCK.

WHO'S THERE?

TANK.

TANK WHO?

YOU'RE WELCOME.

Knock, knock.

Who's there?

Hugo.

Hugo who?

Hugo jump in the lake.

Knock, knock.

Who's there?

Luke.

Luke who?

Luke before you leap.

Knock, knock.

Who's there?

Andrew.

Andrew who?

Andrew on the wall, and she is in trouble!

Knock, knock.

Who's there?

Ears.

Ears who?

Ears looking at you, kid.

Knock, knock.

Who's there?

Cash.

Cash who?

Cash me if you can.

KNOCK, KNOCK.
WHO'S THERE?
KANGA.
KANGA WHO?
NO. KANGAROO!

Knock, knock.

Who's there?

Tuna.

Tuna who?

Tuna your radio down.
I can't get to sleep!

Knock, knock.

Who's there?

Amanda.

Amanda who?

Amanda fix the refrigerator.

Knock, knock.

Who's there?

Wood.

Wood who?

Wood you like to go to a movie?

Knock, knock.

Who's there?

Arthur.

Arthur who?

Arthur any cookies left?

KNOCK, KNOCK.
WHO'S THERE?
LETTUCE.
LETTUCE WHO?
LETTUCE IN.
IT'S HOT OUT HERE!

Knock, knock.

Who's there?

Major.

Major who?

Major open the door, didn't I?

Knock, knock.

Who's there?

Needle.

Needle who?

Needle little help?

Knock, knock.

Who's there?

Sherwood.

Sherwood who?

Sherwood like to come inside.

Knock, knock.

Who's there?

Pasta.

Pasta who?

Pasta salt please.

Knock, knock.

Who's there?

Pudding.

Pudding who?

Pudding on your shoes before your socks is a bad idea.

Knock, knock.

Who's there?

Gopher.

Gopher who?

Gopher help. I'm stuck in the mud!

Knock, knock.

Who's there?

Ash.

Ash who?

Ash sure could use some help painting the house.

Knock, knock.

Who's there?

Who.

Who who?

Do you have an owl in there?

Knock, knock.

Who's there?

Stan.

Stan who?

Stan back. I think I'm going to sneeze!

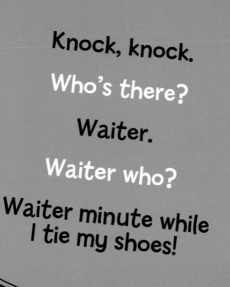

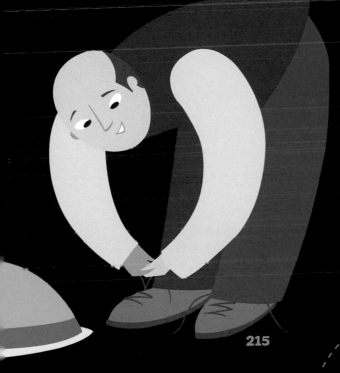

Knock, knock.

Who's there?

Marsha.

Marsha who?

Marshamallow.

Knock, knock.

Who's there?

Orange juice.

Orange juice who?

Orange juice going to let me in?

217

Knock, knock.

Who's there?

Gus.

Gus who?

Gus who's coming to dinner?

Pepper

Knock, knock.

Who's there?

Sultan.

Sultan who?

Sultan Pepper.

Knock, knock.

Who's there?

Olive.

Olive who?

Olive right next door to you.

Knock, knock.

Who's there?

Stopwatch.

Stopwatch who?

Stopwatch you're doing and let me in!

Knock, knock.

Who's there?

Zookeeper.

Zookeeper who?

Zookeeper away from me!

Knock, knock.

Who's there?

Lena.

Lena who?

Lena little closer, and I'll tell you.

Knock, knock.

Who's there?

Alaska.

Alaska who?

Alaska my mom if you can come over.

Knock, knock.

Who's there?

Lenny.

Lenny who?

Lenny give you a kiss.

Knock, knock.

Who's there?

Duck.

Duck who?

Duck! The neighbors are throwing snowballs!

Knock, knock.

Who's there?

Noah.

Noah who?

Noah good place to play ball?

Knock, knock.

Who's there?

Police.

Police who?

Police open up. It's cold out here!

Knock, knock.

Who's there?

Cotton.

Cotton who?

Cotton a trap. Please help me!